Let's Investigate

Habitats and Food Chains

by Ruth Owen

Ruby Tuesday Books

Published in 2017 by Ruby Tuesday Books Ltd.

Editor: Mark J. Sachner
Designer: Emma Randall
Consultant: Judy Wearing, PhD, BEd
Production: John Lingham

Photo credits:
Alamy: 5 (top), 10 (bottom), 21 (bottom left), 26; FLPA: 5 (bottom), 9 (top), 14 (top), 15 (left), 16, 17 (bottom), 23, 31 (top); Istock Photo: 17 (top), 27 (top); Nature Picture Library: 8 (top), 25 (center); Photoshot: 20 (top); Science Photo Library: 19; Shutterstock: Cover, 1, 2–3, 4, 6–7, 8 (bottom), 9 (bottom), 10 (top), 11, 12–13, 14 (bottom), 15 (right), 18, 20 (bottom), 22, 24, 25 (top), 25 (bottom), 27 (bottom), 28–29, 30, 31 (bottom).

Library of Congress Control Number: 2016918443

ISBN 978-1-911341-37-6

Printed and published in the United States of America

For further information including rights and permissions requests, please contact our Customer Service Department at 877-337-8577.

Contents

Words shown in **bold** in the text are explained in the glossary.

The download button shows there are free worksheets or other resources available. Go to:

www.rubytuesdaybooks.com/getstarted

What Is a Habitat?

What do a garden, a forest, and a desert have in common? They are all types of habitats.

Snail

A habitat is a natural **environment** that is home to plants, animals, and other living things.

The living things in a garden get what they need to live from their habitat.

Robin

This robin is eating a worm that it's pulled from a lawn in a garden.

Squirrel

Let's Talk

What do you think plants and animals need from their habitat?

A Garden Habitat

You might not notice the soil in a garden, but without it the plants would have nowhere to grow.

Soil

Lettuce plants

Plants take in water and **nutrients** from soil through their roots.

Lawn

1 inch (2.5 cm)

A lawn isn't just one plant. In a square of lawn this big, there are up to 10 individual grass plants.

Plants make food for
energy inside their leaves.

To do this, they need
air and sunshine.

 **Explore!**

Make a map of a yard or your
school playground.

Gather your equipment:
- Paper with small squares
- Colored pencils
- Camera or phone

1. Begin by using big steps to measure the
   size of the yard. Using your measurements,
   draw the edges of the yard. Each step will
   be one square on the paper.

2. Now draw the yard's trees, grass, and
   other plants on the map. Also add details
   such as paths, a shed, or a patio.

3. Go on a wildlife treasure hunt. When you
   see a bird, snail, bee, or other animal, add
   an X on the map in the place where you
   spotted it.

4. Draw the animals or take a photo of them.
   You can also make a tally chart.

Where did you see the most animals?
Why do you think this is?

Did you spot an animal eating?

Did you find a nest or animal home?

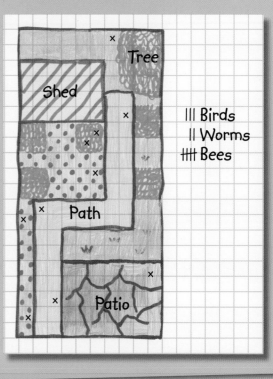

Garden Homes

Beneath the lawn, ants have dug a nest in the soil.

Ant

Ant nest

Young ants called larvae

At night, slugs slither through the garden, eating plants.

By day, they hide in dark, damp places, such as under flowerpots.

Slug

This hedgehog has made a nest under a garden shed.

Hedgehog

The sleepy animal is returning home after a night of hunting for slugs, snails, and worms.

Slug

Hedgehogs are **nocturnal** animals. This means they are active at night and they sleep during the day.

Animals in a garden get the water and food they need from their habitat.

Birds feed on insects and seeds.

Sunflower seeds

Foxes hunt for mice, rabbits, and other small animals. They also steal scraps of food from bird tables and garbage cans.

Fox

What Is a Food Chain?

A food chain is a way to show what the plants and animals in a habitat eat.

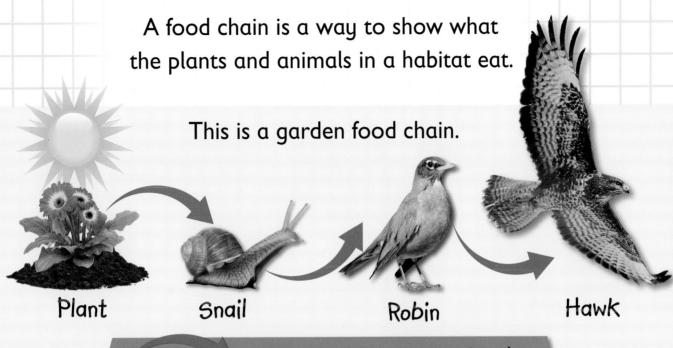

This is a garden food chain.

Plant   Snail   Robin   Hawk

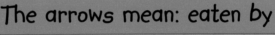

The arrows mean: eaten by

We say a plant is a producer because it uses sunlight to produce its own food.

An animal is a consumer because it eats, or consumes, plants or other animals.

This is another garden food chain.

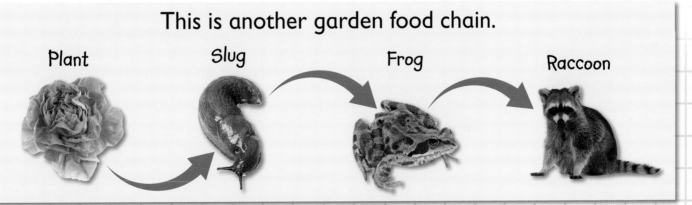

Plant   Slug   Frog   Raccoon

A forest is a habitat where lots of trees grow closely together.

In a forest, you might spot these tree leaves.

Beech

Oak

Maple

A pine tree has thin, needle-like leaves.

Some forests have deciduous trees, such as oaks and beeches, that drop their leaves in autumn.

Some forests have evergreen trees, such as pine trees, that have leaves all year round.

Evergreen trees

Ferns

Ferns and other small plants that like to live in damp, shady habitats grow on the forest floor.

Who Eats Who?

In a forest, worms feed on dead leaves that fall from trees.

Worm

Shrews, mice, toads, birds, and other forest animals feed on worms.

Shrew

Woodpecker

Woodpeckers hunt for ants, termites, and other insects that live in tree bark.

Owls swoop through the trees hunting for shrews, mice, rats, squirrels, rabbits, and small birds.

Owl

Eastern screech owl

Mouse

Shrew

Worm

Leaves

Let's Talk

How do you think a tree trunk is useful to a screech owl?

15

A Forest Nest

A screech owl lays her eggs in a hole in a tree trunk.

Owlet

Fluffy chicks, called owlets, hatch from the eggs. The parent owls bring the owlets small animals to eat.

Let's Talk

You might spot these animals in a forest.

What do you think they are?

What do you think they eat?

You might see this object on the ground in a forest.

What do you think it is?

(The answers to the questions are at the bottom of the page.)

Answers: The animals are caterpillars. They will become moths known as robin moths. The caterpillars feed on leaves. The object is an owl pellet. After an owl has swallowed an animal whole, it later spits out the bones, teeth, and fur in a lump. This lump is called a pellet.

17

Micro-Habitats

Within a large habitat there are lots of small micro-habitats.

Moss

This rotting tree stump is a micro-habitat in a forest.

It is home to small animals and tiny plants, such as moss.

Millions of tiny animals called tardigrades may live in the moss on a tree stump.

They feed on juices from the moss.

Tardigrade

This picture of a tardigrade was taken by a **microscope**. In real life, the little animal is smaller than a grain of sugar.

A Tree Stump Habitat

Look under a rotting log, and you might see woodlice, centipedes, beetles, and spiders.

Woodlouse

Centipede

Woodlice feed on dead or rotting plants. Centipedes are fast-moving hunters that feed on woodlice and small insects.

A Tree Stump Food Chain

Rotting wood   Woodlouse   Centipede   Mouse

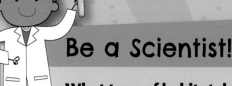

Be a Scientist!

What type of habitat does a woodlouse prefer?

Gather your equipment:
- A small jar, spoon, and paintbrush
- 12 woodlice
- A shoebox
- Cotton balls
- Water
- Pebbles
- Plastic wrap
- A notebook and pen

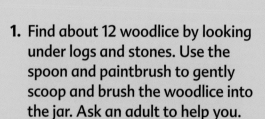

1. Find about 12 woodlice by looking under logs and stones. Use the spoon and paintbrush to gently scoop and brush the woodlice into the jar. Ask an adult to help you.

2. Prepare four different habitats in the shoebox:
   - Wet cotton with pebbles on top
   - Dry cotton with pebbles on top
   - Wet cotton
   - Dry cotton

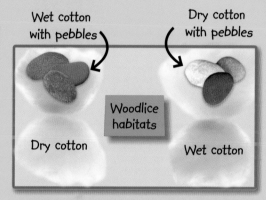

Wet cotton with pebbles

Dry cotton with pebbles

Woodlice habitats

Dry cotton

Wet cotton

Which corner, or habitat, do you think the woodlice will prefer? Why? Write your ideas in a notebook.

3. Gently place the woodlice in the box and cover the box with plastic wrap.

4. Observe the woodlice to see what they do. After 30 minutes, check the four habitats.

Which habitat was most popular?

Do the results match your ideas?

What do the results tell you about woodlice?

5. Carefully return the woodlice to the place where you found them.

(There are some answers at the bottom of the page.)

Answers: The woodlice probably hid in the wet cotton with pebbles on top. This is because woodlice prefer to live in dark, damp habitats, such as under stones and logs.

A Tide Pool Habitat

Peek into a tide pool at the beach, and you're exploring a micro-habitat.

Tide pool

Seaweed

Green, red, and brown seaweed clings to the rocks in the pool.

Seaweed looks like a plant, but it's actually **algae**. Like plants, seaweeds use sunlight to make their own food.

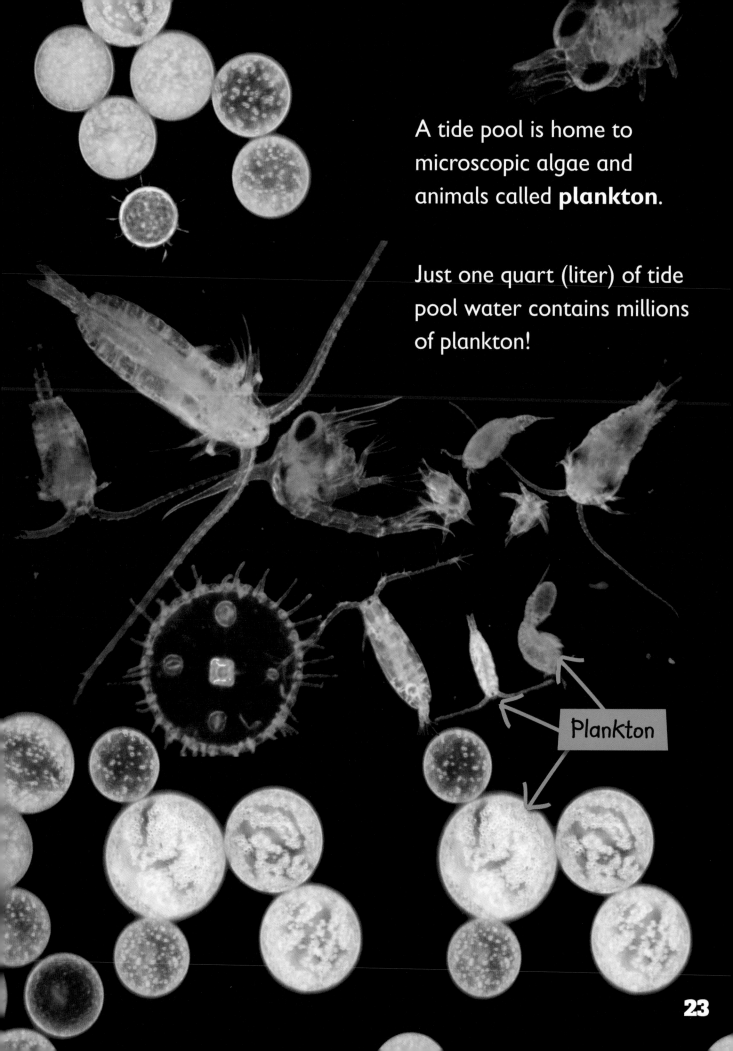

A tide pool is home to microscopic algae and animals called **plankton**.

Just one quart (liter) of tide pool water contains millions of plankton!

Plankton

Tide Pool Creatures

Mussels, limpets, and tiny barnacles cling to the rocks that form the edge of a tide pool.

Mussels

Barnacles

Limpets

Limpet shells

Once the tide comes in, the rocks and animals are covered by seawater.

Limpets move around underwater feeding on seaweed.

Mussels and barnacles eat plankton that's floating in the water.

Trapdoors

Barnacles

Legs

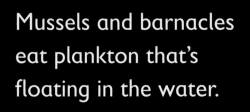

Barnacle

Once it's underwater, a barnacle opens two tiny trapdoors in its shell. It grabs plankton from the water with its legs.

Let's Talk

What do you think has happened to these barnacles?

25

Tide Pool Hunters

Tide pool **predators**, such as dog whelks and starfish, hunt for **prey** such as barnacles and mussels.

Dog whelk

Empty barnacle shells

A dog whelk makes a hole in a barnacle's shell with a hard body part called a radula.

Then the whelk feeds on the soft barnacle inside.

How Does a Starfish Eat a Mussel?

A starfish's mouth is on its underside.

Starfish

Mussel

Tiny feet pull open the mussel's shell.

The starfish pushes its own stomach out through its mouth and into the mussel's shell.

Juices from the starfish's stomach turn the mussel into a soupy meal!

A Tide Pool Food Chain

Plankton

Mussel

Starfish

Seagull

A Desert Habitat

A desert is a habitat where very little rain or snow falls.

In the Sonoran Desert, the weather can be very dry and scorching hot.

Cactus

Fat, round stem

Plants called cacti grow in this desert.

When it rains, a cactus takes in water through its roots.

It stores the water in its stems—sometimes for years!

Saguaro cactus

Birds, bats, and insects feed on sweet **nectar** from a saguaro's flowers.

Most cacti have sharp spines.

Stems

A large saguaro cactus that's full of water may weigh as much as an elephant.

Desert Survival

How do animals survive in the Sonoran Desert?

Desert tortoise

It's so hot in summer that a desert tortoise stays underground in a burrow.

The tortoise doesn't eat or drink for several months.

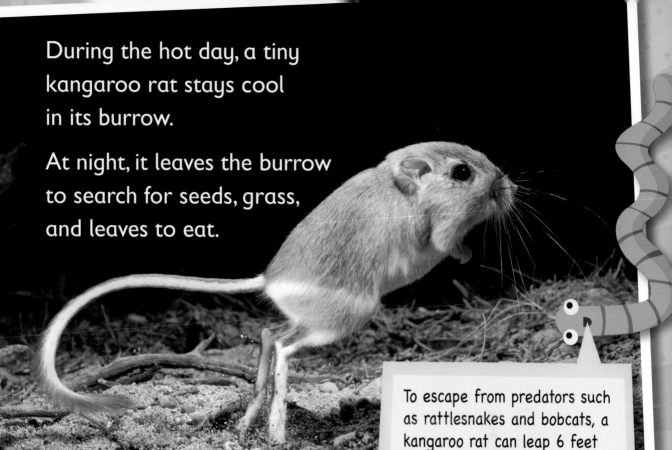

During the hot day, a tiny kangaroo rat stays cool in its burrow.

At night, it leaves the burrow to search for seeds, grass, and leaves to eat.

To escape from predators such as rattlesnakes and bobcats, a kangaroo rat can leap 6 feet (1.8 m) in a single hop.

Let's Draw It!

Can you put these living things in the correct order to make a desert food chain?

Draw and label your food chain.

(The answer is at the bottom of the page.)

Kangaroo rat

Plants

Bobcat

Rattlesnake

Glossary

algae (AL-gee)
Plant-like living things that mostly grow and live in water.

environment (en-VYE-ruhn-muhnt)
The place where animals, plants, and other living things make their home, and all the things, such as air, weather, and soil, that affect them.

microscope (MYE-kruh-skope)
A piece of equipment used for seeing things that are too small to see with your eyes alone.

nectar (NEK-tur)
A sweet liquid made by flowers.

nocturnal (nok-TUR-nuhl)
Only active at night. Nocturnal animals sleep during the day.

nutrient (NOO-tree-uhnt)
A substance that a living thing needs to grow and be healthy.

plankton (PLANGK-tuhn)
Microscopic living things, such as animals and algae, that float in water.

predator (PRED-uh-tur)
An animal that hunts and eats other animals.

prey (PRAY)
An animal that is hunted by other animals for food.

Index